Table of Contents

Chapter One 16
Set up your phone 16
Charge the device battery 17
Turn on your device 17
Use the Setup Wizard 18
Import data from an old device 18
Lock or unlock 19
Accounts 20
    Add a Google Account 20
    Add a Samsung account 20
    Add an Outlook account 21
    Set up voicemail 21
Navigation 22
Navigation bar 25
    Navigation buttons 25
    Navigation gestures 26
Customize your home screen 27
    App icons 27
    Wallpaper 27
    Themes 28
    Icons 29
    Widgets 29

Customize widgets 30
Status bar 31
　　Status icons 31
Notification panel 32
　　View the notification panel 32
Chapter Two 34
Biometric security 34
　　Face recognition 34
　　Face recognition management 35
　　Fingerprint scanner 35
　　Fingerprint management 36
　　Biometrics settings 36
Mobile continuity 37
　　Call and text on other devices 37
Multi window 38
　　Window controls 39
Edge panels 40
　　Apps panel 40
　　Configure Edge panels 41
Enter text 43
　　Toolbar 43
　　Configure the Samsung keyboard 44
Chapter Three 47

Camera and Gallery 47
    Camera 47
    Navigate the camera screen 48
    Configure shooting mode 49
    Record videos 51
    Camera settings 52
    Gallery 55
    View pictures 55
    Edit pictures 56
    Play video 57
    Edit video 58
    Share pictures and videos 58
    Delete pictures and videos 59
Take a screenshot 60
    Screenshot settings 60
Chapter Four 61
Applications 61
    Uninstall or disable apps 61
    Search for apps 61
    Sort apps 62
    Create and use folders 63
    Copy a folder to a Home screen 64
    Delete a folder 64

App settings 64
Chapter Five 66
Contacts 66
    Create a contact 66
    Edit a contact 67
    Favorites 67
    Share a contact 68
Groups 69
    Create a group 69
    Add or remove group contacts 70
    Send a message to a group 70
    Send an email to a group 71
    Delete a group 71
    Merge contacts 72
    Delete duplicate contacts 73
    Import contacts 73
    Export contacts 74
    Sync contacts 74
    Delete contacts 75
Chapter Six 76
Internet 76
    Browser tabs 76
    Create a Bookmark 77

- Open a Bookmark 77
- Save a web page 77
- View history 78
- Share pages 78
- Secret mode 79
  - Secret mode settings 79
  - Turn off secret mode 80
- Messages 81
  - Message search 82
  - Delete conversations 82
  - Send SOS messages 83
  - Message settings 84
  - Emergency alerts 84
- My Files 85
  - File groups 85
  - My Files options 86
- Chapter Seven 88
- Phone 88
  - Calls 88
  - Make a call 88
  - Make a call from Recent 89
  - Make a call from Contacts 89
  - Answer a call 89

- Decline a call ... 90
- Decline with a message ... 90
- End a call ... 90
- Actions while on a call ... 91
- Switch to headset or speaker ... 91
- Multitask ... 92
- Call background ... 92
- Call pop-up settings ... 93
- Manage calls ... 94
- Call log ... 94
- Save a contact from a recent call ... 94
- Delete call records ... 95
- Block a number ... 95
- Speed dial ... 96
- Make a call with Speed dial ... 97
- Remove a Speed dial number ... 97
- Emergency calls ... 98
- Phone settings ... 98
- Optional calling services ... 99
- Place a multi-party call ... 99
- Video calls ... 99
- Real Time Text (RTT) ... 100
- Samsung Health ... 101

Before you start exercising 101
Settings 103
Access Settings 103
    Search for Settings 103
Chapter Eight 104
Connections 104
Wi-Fi 104
    Connect to a hidden Wi-Fi network 104
    Advanced Wi-Fi settings 105
    Wi-Fi Direct 107
    Disconnect from Wi-Fi Direct 107
Bluetooth 108
    Rename a paired device 108
    Un-pair from a Bluetooth device 109
    Advanced options 109
NFC and payment 111
    Tap and pay 111
Airplane mode 112
Mobile networks 112
Data usage 114
    Turn on Data saver 114
    Monitor mobile data 115
    Monitor Wi-Fi data 116

- Mobile hotspot 116
  - Configure mobile hotspot settings 117
  - Auto hotspot 117
  - Tethering 118
- Connect to a printer 118
- Virtual Private Networks 119
  - Manage a VPN 119
  - Connect to a VPN 120
- Private DNS 121
- Ethernet 121
- Sounds and vibration 122
  - Sound mode 122
  - Vibrations 122
  - Volume 123
  - Media volume limit 124
  - Ringtone 124
  - Notification sound 125
  - System sounds and vibration 125
- Do not disturb 127
  - Alert when phone picked up 128
  - Turn over to mute 128
- Chapter Nine 130
- Display 130

Dark mode 130
Screen brightness 131
Motion smoothness.. 131
Eye comfort shield... 132
Font size and style... 132
Screen zoom 133
Full screen apps 133
Screen timeout 133
Touch sensitivity 134
Screen saver 134
Lift to wake 135
Double tap to turn on screen..................................... 135
Double tap to turn off screen 136
Keep screen on while viewing 136
One-handed mode 136

Lock screen and security 137
Screen lock types 137
Set a secure screen lock 137

Clock and information 139

Find My Mobile 140
Turn on Find My Mobile... 140

Find My Device 142

Secure Folder... 143

Private Share 143

Install unknown apps 144

Encrypt or decrypt SD card 144

Decrypt SD card 145

Password for factory data reset 145

Set up SIM card lock 146

View passwords 146

Device administration 147

Credential storage 147

Permission manager 148

Samsung Privacy 149

Date and time 149

Reset 150

    Reset all settings 150

    Reset network settings 151

    Reset accessibility settings 151

    Auto restart at set times 151

    Factory Data Reset 152

Google Device Protection 153

    Enable Google Device Protection 153

    Disable Google Device Protection 153

Introduction

The Samsung Galaxy A15 is a special smartphone that offers several mind-blowing features. Within the pages of this manual, you'll discover everything you need to know that will enable you use the device with confidence and ease.

This guide exposes all the hidden feature of the Samsung Galaxy A15.

As a beginner or senior user this book will improve your smartphone experience and make you a true master of the Galaxy A15.

This book is suitable to users of all levels.

Copyright 2024 © Michael Donald

All rights reserved. This book is copyrighted and no part of it may be reproduced, stored, or transmitted, in any form or means, without the prior written permission of the copyright owner. Printed in the United States of America.

Copyright 2024 © Michael Donald

Galaxy A15 Layout

Chapter One
Set up your phone

The Nano-SIM card is an accessory used by your device. SIM cards may be preinstalled, or your previous SIM may be acceptable.

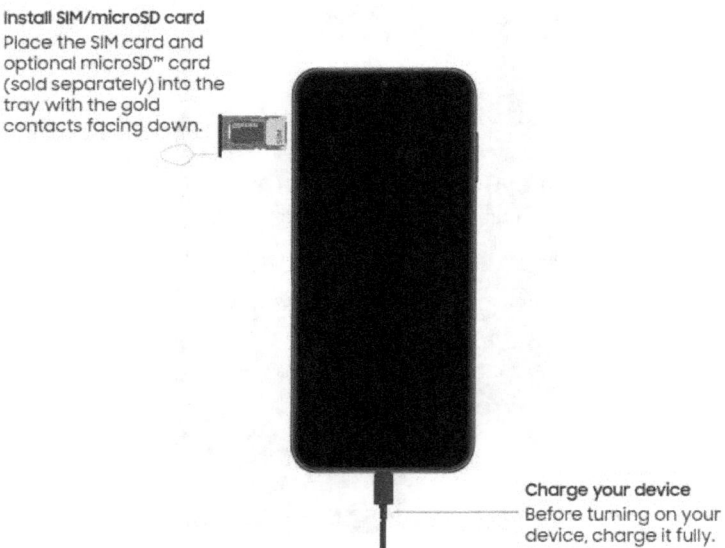

Install SIM/microSD card
Place the SIM card and optional microSD™ card (sold separately) into the tray with the gold contacts facing down.

Charge your device
Before turning on your device, charge it fully.

TIP: Only Samsung approved cables, battery, chargers and other accessories are to be used on your device, using unapproved accessories may cause damages to the device and take note that warranty does not cover damages cause by user misuse.

Charge the device battery

The Galaxy A15 is be made up of a powerful rechargeable battery.

NOTE: While the charging is going on, the charger may overheat and stop working, this does not affect the lifespan of the phone, all you need to do is to detach the charger from the device and wait for it to cool down.

Turn on your device

Use the Side key to turn on the device. Device with a cracked or broken body should not be used until it is fixed.

- o Pressing and holding the Side key for few seconds to turn on the device.
- • After pressing and holding the Side key, tap the ⏻ Power off icon on the screen to turn off the device.
- • After pressing and holding the Side key, tap the ↻ Restart icon on the screen to restart the device.

Use the Setup Wizard

The Setup Wizard directs you on how to setup the smartphone when you turn it on for the first time.

In order to change default language, setup an account, connecting to a Wi-Fi network and more tag alongside the instruction displayed on the screen.

Import data from an old device

Data and files like contacts, photos, videos, calendars, messages, notes and music can be transferred between devices with the help of the Smart Switch. You might have Smart Switch on your device, but if you don't have you can download it. Data can be transferred via Smart Switch using a USB cable, Wi-Fi, or computer.

1. Enter Settings application, press 🔄 Accounts and backup menu and tap Bring data from old device.
2. After performing the action above, follow the on-screen directives.

Lock or unlock

The lock screen automatically locks when the screen times out. Press the Side key to manually lock and unlock the device.

Side key/Fingerprint scanner
Press to lock.
Press to turn on the screen, and then swipe the screen to unlock it.

Accounts

Create and manage account.

Add a Google Account

You may be denied access to your Google Cloud Storage if you didn't log in to your Google account.

Logging into your Google account and setting up a lock screen will automatically enable "Google Device Protection".

1. Launch settings app on the device and then select ⟳ Accounts and backup > Manage accounts.
2. To add a Google account, select Google under the ✛ Add account menu.

Add a Samsung account

You will be able to access Samsung exclusive contents fully when sign in your Samsung account on the device.

- Open setting application on your device and then select Samsung account.

Add an Outlook account

When signed in, you can view and control emails.

1. Enter setting app on the device and then select ⟳Accounts and backup menu > tap Manage accounts.
2. To add an outlook account, select Outlook under the ✚ Add account.

Set up voicemail

In order to use voicemail feature, you must set it up when accessing it for the first time. Voicemail can be accessed from Phone app.

1. Launch 🅲 Phone from the Apps screen, touch 📧 Voicemail or press and hold 1∞ button.
2. Follow the directives displayed on the screen to create a password, record your name or greeting.

Navigation

To navigate on the screen, you don't need to apply excess pressure or metal objects on the screen. Using metallic object or excess pressure on the screen may cause damage to the device and warranty doesn't cover such damages.

Tap

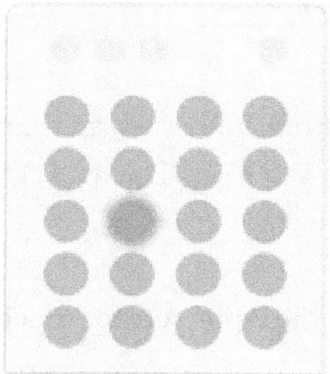

Gently tap an item to launch it.

- Click an item to select it.
- To zoom in or out on an image, click on the image twice.

Swipe

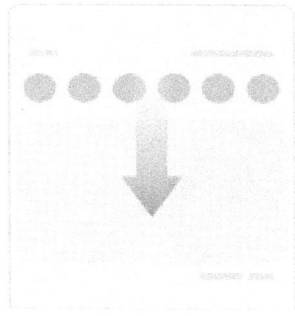

To use the swipe feature, drag your finger across the screen.

- To unlock the device, swipe upward from the bottom of the lock screen.

Drag and drop

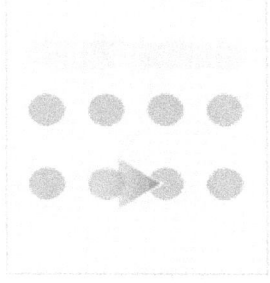

To change to location of an item simply tap and hold the item and then move it to a new place.

- In order to add an application shortcut to the home screen, drag the shortcut to the home screen.

Zoom in and out

- Spread your fingers apart to zoom in.
- Join your finger together to zoom out.

Touch and hold

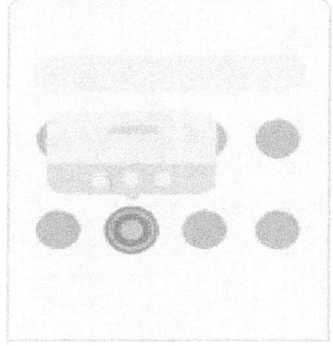

To activate items, all you need do is press and hold them.

- To make change to your Home screen just press and hold a blank space and choose the options you want to use.

Navigation bar

The navigation buttons or the full screen gesture can be used to navigate on the device.

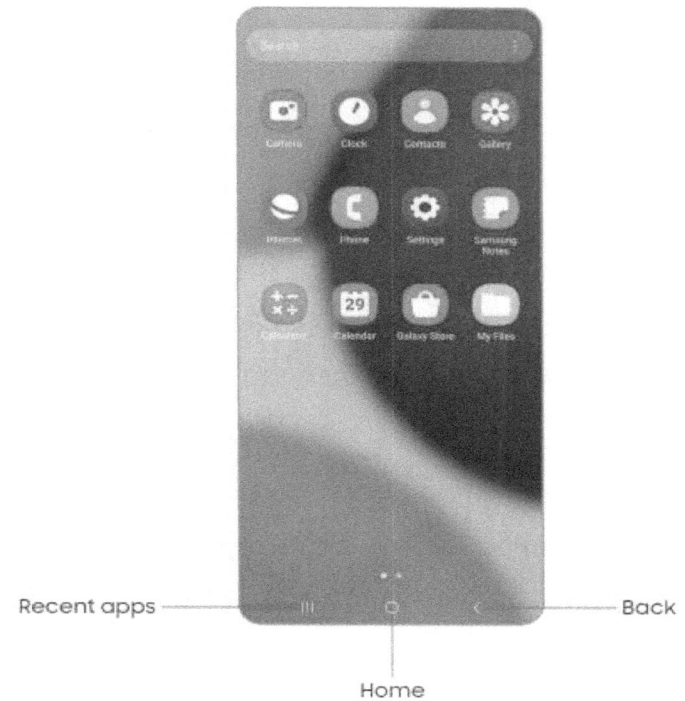

Recent apps — Back — Home

Navigation buttons

To easily navigate on the device, simply touch the button at the bottom screen.

1. Launch setting application and then select Display > Navigation bar > Buttons.

2. In order to set how the Back, Home and Recent button should display on the screen, tap **Button order**.

Navigation gestures

Hide the navigation buttons and activate navigation gestures so you can navigate by swiping on the screen.

Do the following:

1. Enter Settings page, select Display, tap Navigation bar and then tap Swipe gestures to enable the feature.
2. Select an option to customize:
- More options: Tap more options button to select a gesture type and sensitivity.
- Gesture hints: With this feature, you can make lines appears at the bottom screen where each gesture is located.
- Display button to hide keyboard: When your device is in Portrait mode, display an icon on the bottom right corner of your screen to hide the keyboard.

Customize your home screen

To create a better Home screen experience, add frequently used apps and widgets to your Home screen.

App icons

You can launch applications from your Home screen by clicking on their icons.

- From the App screen, select ⌂ Add to Home after pressing and holding the application icon.

To delete an application icon:

- The delete button 🗑 will appear when you press and hold the application you want to remove from the Home screen.

NOTE: Apps that are removed from the Home screen are not uninstalled from the device.

Wallpaper

Apply system wallpapers or your own picture as a background image.

Do the following to apply a background image:

1. Go to the Home screen page, press and hold an empty space then tap 🖼 Wallpapers & style.

2. Choose one of the following options to view available wallpapers:
- Click the Home screen and lock screen image to customize them.
- Browse my wallpapers: Select a background from the default wallpapers or download from Galaxy Themes.
- Color palette: You can choose a palette to match the color on your wallpaper.
- Apply dark mode to wallpaper: Tap dark mode and then follow the instruction on the screen to apply dark mode to wallpaper.

Themes

You can download a theme and apply it as your App icons, Home screen, Wallpapers and Lock screen.

1. Press and hold a space from the Home screen.
2. Tap to select theme. Preview the theme you want before downloading it.
3. To view the themes you have downloaded, tap , select My stuff >Themes.
4. To apply a theme, select it and touch apply.

Icons

You can download icons to replace the default system icons.

1. Hold anyplace on the Home screen.
2. Press ![] Themes > Icons, select a set of icons and then download it.
3. To view the icons you have downloaded, select ![] >My stuff > Icons.
4. To apply the selected icon, tap Apply.

Widgets

You can Add widget to the home screen by following the instructions below:

1. Press and hold a space with no item in the Home screen.
2. Click a set of widgets to open it after tapping ![].
3. After choosing a widget, tap **Add** to apply it on the Home screen.

Customize widgets

You can customize the widgets function on the Home screen.

- o Press and hold the widget you want to edit on the Home screen and select one of the options below:

    - ⊞ Create stack: You can add other widgets of the same size to stack in same position on the Home screen.

    - 🗑 Remove: To remove a widget from the Home screen, tap the Remove button.

    - ⚙ Settings: Modify widgets appearance on the Home screen.

    - ⓘ App info: If you want to view more info about a particular widget, hold the widget then tap App info button.

Status bar

On the status bar, you can quickly access the status icons and notification icons. The icons below are available in status bar.

Status icons

Notification icons

NOTE: If you want to modify the status bar, enter Quick settings, select ⋮More > Status.

Notification panel

The notification panel is where you can quickly access settings, notification and more.

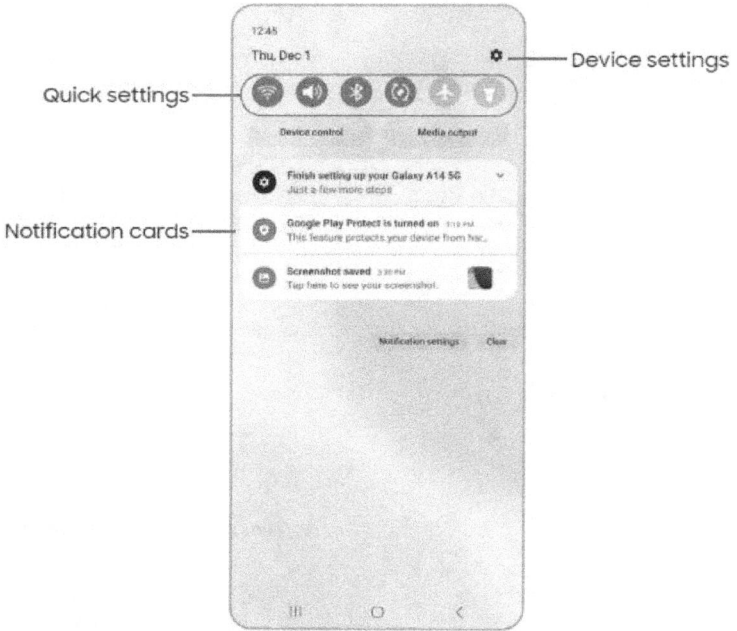

View the notification panel

Swipe down to access the notifications panel.

1. From the top screen, swipe down to enter the notification panel page.

- Click on the desired notification you want to view.

- Drag the notification the lefts or right side of the notification panel to remove it.
- To delete all the notification on the Notification panel, select **Clear**.
- To edit a single notification, select **Notification settings**.

2. To leave the Notification panel page select Back.

Chapter Two
Biometric security

You can sign in to accounts securely and unlock your phone using this feature.

Face recognition

Set up this feature, so that your device will automatically unlock when you look at it.

NOTE: You will have to set up a PIN, Password or Pattern before you will be allowed to use this feature.

- If you need a stronger security of your device the Pattern, PIN or Password is more secure to unlock your device compare to face recognition.
- Anyone that looks like you can unlock your device.
- Face recognition can be affected with these factors; Wearing of glasses, heavy make-up, beards or hats
- Clean your camera lens and enroll your face in a well-lit background.//
1. Open setting application, press ⬤ Security and privacy > Biometrics then tap Face recognition.

2. Instruction will appear on the screen to guide you on how to enroll your face.

Face recognition management

1. Enter settings, tap ⭕ Security and privacy > Biometrics then tap Face recognition.
   - The existing face data can be deleted.
   - Add an optional appearance to improve the performance of the face recognition.
   - The face recognition security can be deactivated.
   - When in an area with low light, increase the screen brightness so that the device can detect your face.

Fingerprint scanner

The fingerprint validation is also another security feature which enables you to unlock the device and sign in to your Samsung account.

NOTE: Before this feature can be used on your device you must set a Pattern, PIN or password.

1. On settings page, press ⭕ Security and privacy > Biometrics and then tap Face recognition.

2. Instruction will display on the screen to guide you on how to enroll your fingerprint.

Fingerprint management

1. On settings, select ⬤ Security and privacy > Biometrics then tap Fingerprints. The options under are available:

- To rename or delete a fingerprint, select it.
- To add another fingerprint, select Add fingerprint. Instruction will appear on the screen to guide you on how to add fingerprint.
- Scan a fingerprint to see if it has been fully registered.

Biometrics settings

1. On settings page, press ⬤ Security & Privacy > Biometrics.

- When using biometric to unlock the device, you can set to display a transition effect.

Mobile continuity

Using mobile continuity, you can access your device storage on another mobile device or computer.

Call and text on other devices

When you sign in to your Samsung account, you can make and receive calls and SMS messages from your Galaxy devices.

1. On Settings, press Connected devices > Call & text on other devices.
2. Press to make this feature active.
3. On your Galaxy device, log in to your Samsung account.

Multi window

Multitask by running multiple apps simultaneously. Apps that support multi windows can be displayed on a split screen. You can switch between apps and adjust the size of their windows.

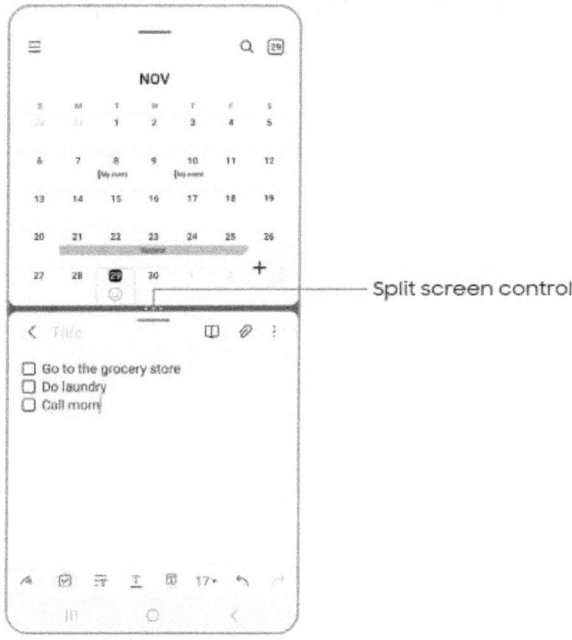

1. From any screen you are in select the button for Recent.

2. Select the icon for the app you want to open in the split screen view.

3. To add an app to the split screen view, select the app in another widow.

- To change the sizes of the window, drag the margin.

Window controls

This feature modifies the way application windows are shown in split screen view.

1. To adjust the size of the app window, drag the middle of the window margin.
2. To access the options that will be shown below, touch the center of the window margin:

- Touch the ↑↓ icon to switch between two windows.

- Touch the ⊞ icon to add an app pair shortcut to the Apps panel or Edge panel.

Edge panels

From the Edge panels, you can access apps, contacts, tasks, and news from Edge panels, as well as view sports and news from the edges of the screen.

The following should be done if you want to activate the edge panel:

- While on the Settings page, select ⚙ Display > Edge panels, touch ⬤ to activate the feature.

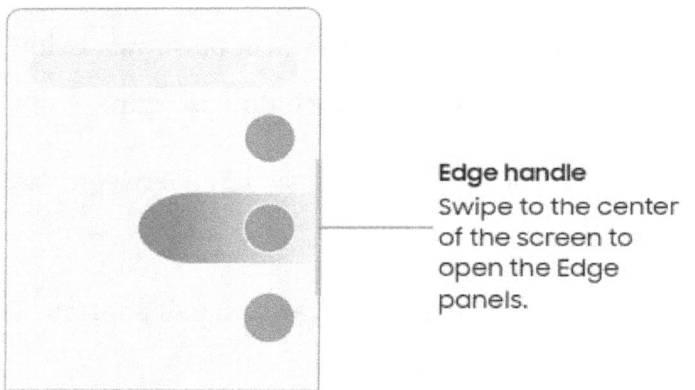

Edge handle
Swipe to the center of the screen to open the Edge panels.

Apps panel

Applications can be added into two columns in the apps panel.

1. The edge handle should be taken to the middle of the screen. Continue swiping until the Apps panel appear

2. To launch an app select it. Click ⋮⋮ All apps to view the full app list

To configure Apps panel:

1. Pull the Edge panel to the middle of the screen then swipe until the Apps panel appears.

2. Select the ✎ icon to edit other application to the Apps panel

- Drag the icon of an app to an empty space in the Apps panel to added

- The Apps panel app arrangement can be changed.

- To take out an app from the apps panel, select ▬ Remove.

3. You can save changes you have made by selecting ⟨ Back

Configure Edge panels

The following should be done to make changes to the Edge panels.

1. On settings, press ✸ Display > Edge panels > Panels.

2. The options under are available:

- ✓ Checkbox: The Edge panel can be activated or deactivated.
- Edit (if available): Each panel can be personalized
- 🔍 Search: Use the search feature to find panels.
- ⋮ More settings:

— Reorder: Drag panels to the left or right to rearrange them.

— Uninstall: From your device you can delete panels that were installed.

— Hide on Lock screen: Hide panels from Lock screen.

- Galaxy store: From the Galaxy Store you can download more edge panels.

Enter text

You can either type or use voice to enter text on the Keyboard.

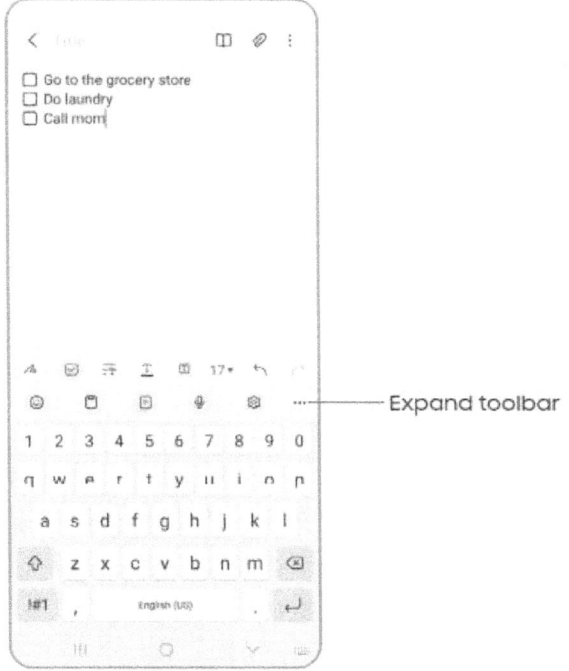

Toolbar

The Emoji, Stickers, Clipboard and Translator are available on the toolbar.

- On the Keyboard, press ••• Expand toolbar to use the following option:

Expression: Explore different types of emojis, GIFs, create custom combined emojis, and more.

Clipboard: Access the clipboard.

One-handed keyboard: Switch to a layout for one-handed use.

Voice input: Use Samsung voice input.

Settings: Access keyboard settings.

Split keyboard: Change the keyboard to a split version that is separated.

Floating keyboard: Change the keyboard to a floating version that can be moved anywhere on the screen.

Search: Locate specific words or phrases in your conversations.

Translate: Type words or sentences in the keyboard to translate them into another language.

Grammarly: Get suggestions from Grammarly as you type.

Emojis: Insert an emoji.

GIFs: Add animated GIFs.

Bitmoji: Create your own personal emoji and use it in stickers.

Mojitok: Create your own stickers or insert automatically suggested ones.

AR Emoji: Create your own personal emoji and use it in stickers you can share.

Keyboard size: Adjust the height and width of the keyboard.

Text editing: Use an editing panel to help pinpoint text that you want to cut, copy, and paste.

Configure the Samsung keyboard

You can customize options for the keyboard.

- o On the keyboard, press Settings, the options under will appear:
- • Languages and types: Choose a language and keyboard style you prefer.

Smart typing

- **Predictive text:** Recommended words and phrases will appear as you type on the Samsung keyboard when you turn on predictive text.
- **Suggested emojis:** Emoji will be suggested to you as you type when predictive text is turned on.
- **Auto replace:** You can replace what you type with predictive text suggestion.
- **Suggest text corrections:** All words that are spelled wrongly will automatically be checked and underlined in red when you turn on this feature.

Style and layout

- **Keyboard toolbar:** The toolbar of the Samsung keyboard can be hidden.
- **High contrast keyboard:** Increase the contrast between the keys and background of the Keyboard.
- **Theme:** Select a preferred keyboard theme.
- **Mode:** You can use either Portrait or Landscape mode for your keyboard.

- **Size and transparency:** Customize the transparency and size the Samsung keyboard.
- **Layout:** Show special character and number on the keyboard.
- **Font size:** Move the slider to customize the font size.

Other settings

- **Voice input:** Modify voice input settings.
- **Reset to default settings:** You can restore the original keyboard setting and remove personalized data.

Chapter Three
Camera and Gallery

Images and videos can be captured using the Camera app and stored in the Gallery where they can be viewed and edited.

Camera

With full-featured pro lenses and video settings and modes, you can make any video look great.

- Launch the ⬤ Camera application.

TIP: From the lock screen push the Side key twice to activate the camera.

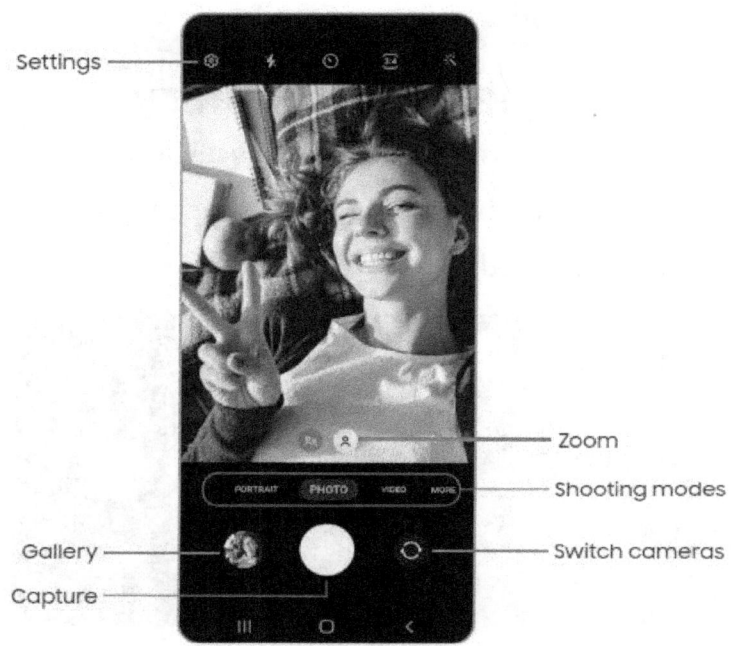

Navigate the camera screen

Your device's front and rear cameras are capable of taking stunning pictures, so take advantage of that.

1. Go to the Apps screen and search for the 📷 Camera app then set up your shots in line with the following features:

- Tap where you want the camera to focus, on the screen.

- The camera screen will display a brightness scale if it is tapped. Move the showing slider to adjust the camera brightness.

- From the camera screen, make a swipe upward or downward to use either the font or the rear camera.

- To change the shooting mode of the camera, make a swipe to the left or right on the camera screen.

- The camera settings can be change from the ⚙ Settings menu.

2. Press ⃝ to take a photo.

Configure shooting mode

Let the camera determine the best shooting mode for your photographs or simply select from a variety of modes.

- o Swipe right or left on the camera screen to manually change the shooting mode.

- Portrait mode: The background of your Portrait images shots can be altered.

- Photo: Just allow the camera app to decide the perfect settings for capturing images.

- Video: Leave the camera app to decide the perfect settings for recording videos.

- More: There are other available shooting modes that can be selected. By tapping ⊕ Add on the Camera app screen, other modes can be dragged in and out of the shooting modes tray which is located at the lower part of the Camera app screen.

  – Deco Pic: Picture that you have already taken can be decorated with the camera.

  – Pro: The ISO sensitivity, exposure value, white balance, and color tone when capturing pictures.

  – Panorama: Capture images either in a horizontal direction or a vertical direction to create a linear image.

  – Food: While this mode is activated, images that lay more emphasis on the vivid color of food can be taken.

- Macro: Image that are in range of 3-5 cm away from you can be taken

Record videos

Make a video recording of ongoing event around you with your device camera.

1. From the camera screen, swipe left or right to change the shooting mode.
2. To start the video recording an event that is ongoing, select ● Record.
- You might want to take an image from your video while the recording is going on, it is simple it's just for you to tap the ⊡ Capture icon
- To have a temporary break on your recording, just simply select the ‖ Pause icon and to resume the same process, click on the ● Record icon again to resume from the temporary break.
3. To end video recording, press the ■ Stop button.

Camera settings

The camera settings will be configured when you follow the steps below.

- The ⚙ Setting icon should be tapped on the 📷 Camera screen so that the following options will appear:

Pictures

- By swiping the shutter button to the nearest edge on the camera screen, you will be able to capture burst shots and also create a GIF as well.

- The HEIF picture format is recommended for you to save pictures so as to save your mobile device storage space.

- Save selfies as previewed: Without flipping (tossing) selfies, they can be saved as previewed (as they appear).

Videos

- High efficiency videos format: Management and conservation of your mobile device storage can be managed by recording videos in the

HEVC format. This playback format may not be supported by all sharing sites.

Useful features

- Auto HDR: The Auto HDR feature enables you to capture information from the dark or bright areas of your shots.

- Grid lines: Set the display view finder grid lines for your photos or videos to be well composed.

- Location tags: GPS location tag can also be added to your images or video for easy tracking.

- Shooting modes:

– The volume keys when pressed, has other functions other than decreasing or increasing the media sound volume; those features include, capturing images, recording videos, zooming in or out and controlling the system sound volume.

– Set up an addition floating shutter button on the screen of your camera app so that you can move it anywhere on the screen.

- Show palm: To have your images capture in few seconds, place your hands out with the palm directed toward the camera lens.
- Settings to be retained: You can decide to launch the camera with the same shooting mode, selfie angle and the filter you used the last time.
- Storage location: Choose a storage location on your device to save your file.
- Watermark: Water marks can be added to your pictures from the bottom left corner of the screen.
- Shutter sound: Go to your camera settings and set your device to make a sound when you press the shutter button.
- Reset settings: Go to your camera settings and return you camera as it was when you first set up the device.

Gallery

You can manage and edit your images and videos by going to the Gallery on your device.

- Launch ✻ Gallery application from the App screen.

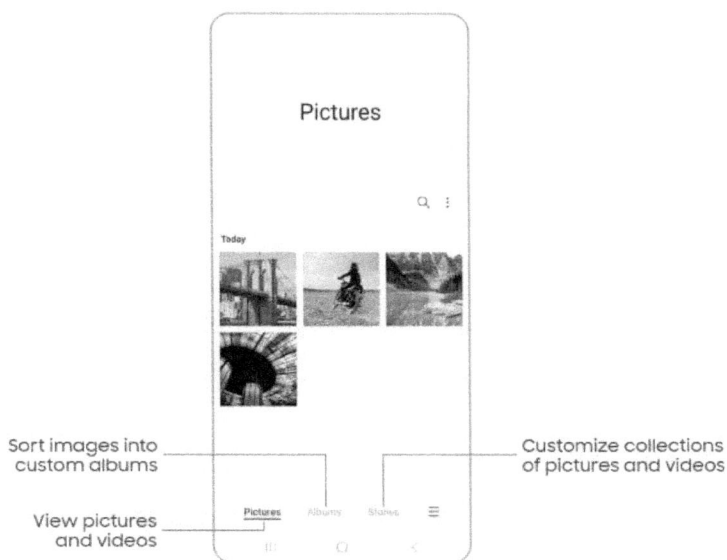

View pictures

A picture stored on your device can be viewed in the Gallery application.

1. Tap ✻ Gallery from the App screen.
2. Click on the picture you want to view.

- To add your best picture to your favorite list, select ♡ Add to Favorites.
- By tapping ⋮ More option, you can access other feature.
  - Details: You will have access to view and edit the photo info.
  - Copy to clipboard: The clipboard stores copied content such as text or images.
  - Set as wallpaper: Create a wallpaper using the picture.
  - Print: Connect a printer to the computer and send the picture there.

Edit pictures

Take advantage of the editing tools available in the Gallery to enhance your pictures.

1. Select Pictures from the ✲ Gallery app.
2. To edit a picture, click on it and then tap ✎.

- ⤵ Transform: Changing the overall appearance of the picture is as simple as rotating, flipping, cropping, or other adjustments.

- ⊙ Filters: Select a filter to add color effects.
- ☼ Tone: Select tone button to adjust the exposure, brightness and contrast.
- ☺ Decorations: You can include text, hand drawn content or stickers.

3. Revert: Restore the default pictures

Play video

You can view your device's videos, save them as favorites, and view details about them.

1. Hit Picture from ✳ Gallery app.
2. To view a video, tap it and swipe left or right.
- To include your Favorite video to the list of favorites, select ♡ Add to favorites.
- The following feature will be accessed when you select ⋮ More:
- Details: The information about the video can be viewed and edited.

- Set as wallpaper: Make the video the lock screen wallpaper by setting it as the background.

3. To watch the video on your Gallery app Press ▶ Play.

Edit video

To edit the video stored on your mobile phone Gallery's app, do the following.

1. Select "Pictures" under ✽ Gallery.
2. Select the video you want to edit to view it.
3. Select ✎ Edit from the video menu to cut segments.
4. After editing the video, select **Save** and confirm.

Share pictures and videos

Your videos and pictures can be shared with friends and family and also across all social media platforms like the Facebook, Twitter, Instagram, Tiktok, and WhatsApp.

1. Hit **Pictures** from the ✽ Gallery application.

2. Press ⋮ More > Edit and choose the image or video you want to send.

3. Click ⤳ Share, and then choose a sharing application or connection.

Delete pictures and videos

On your device, you can delete photos and videos that have been stored there.

1. Go to ✻ Gallery app, press ⋮ more > edit.
2. Press videos and pictures to choose them.
3. After selecting the images and videos to be deleted, select 🗑 Delete icon.

Take a screenshot

With this feature, you can capture an image of your screen and then your mobile device will create a screenshots album in the gallery application.

- o Press the Side and Volume down keys simultaneously to capture a screenshot.

Screenshot settings

Modify the settings of your screenshot.

1. While on the settings application, press Advanced > Screenshots.

- Show toolbar after capturing: Display more options on the screenshot tool bar after capturing a screenshot.
- Delete after sharing from toolbar: You can delete screenshots after they are shared through the screenshot toolbar.
- Hide status and navigation bars: You can set your mobile phone to hide the navigation bar and status on a screenshot.
- Format to save Screenshot: Save pictures in JPG and PNG.

Chapter Four
Applications

From your Apps screen, you will see all downloaded apps. You can set them to appear on the Home screen.

- o To view all apps on the Apps screen, unlock your device and swipe upward from the Home screen.

Uninstall or disable apps

Apps downloaded from the Galaxy store or the Play Store can be uninstalled. The preloaded application can only be disabled.

- o Swipe upward from the Home screen to display the Apps screen then press and hold an app and select either Uninstall or Disable.

Search for apps

The search feature on your mobile phone allows you to look for apps and settings that you are not sure of where to find them.

1. Swipe upward from the Home screen to display the Apps screen then enter a keyword on the

search bar. Apps and settings that matches your search will app as a result as you are typing in the words for your search

2. If the app or setting is found click on it to access it.

NOTE: Go to the More options menu and select the Settings option to customize your search settings.

Sort apps

From the Apps screen you can customize the arrangement of apps and apps shortcut.

- o Swipe up from the Home screen to view the Apps screen then select More options and tap Sort to use the following arrangement options:
- • Apps can be arranged manually in your own preferred manner.
- • You can also decide to sort apps alphabetically which is the default arrangement settings.

NOTE: If apps are manually arranged on the Apps screen, select More options then select Clean up pages, to removed open space.

Create and use folders

Once folders are created on your Apps screen or Home screen they will be easily access and well arranged.

1. To access the Apps screen from the Home screen, unlock your device and swipe upward from the Home screen, then press and hold a shortcut for an app to move it on top of another app until it is highlighted.

2. The folder will automatically be created when you release the app that you placed on top of the other.

- Folder name: Select a name for the folder.

- Palette: Choose a color to use for the folder.

- Add apps: To include apps to the folder that you have created, there is a Plus icon located in the folder, tap it and choose the app you want to add, then select Done

3. To close the folder, select the Back icon.

Copy a folder to a Home screen

A folder can be copied to the Home screen when your do the following:

- o Unlock your mobile phone and swipe upward from the Home screen to access the Apps screen, then press and hold the app you want to add to the home screen and select ⊕ Add to Home.

Delete a folder

When a folder is either delete from the Home screen or the Apps screen all apps shortcuts remains on your device but goes back to the Apps screen.

1. To delete a folder, go to the Apps list, then press and hold the folder you want to delete.
2. After selecting the folder, you want to delete, tap the 🗑 Delete folder icon and confirm the deletion.

App settings

Apps that are either available on your device by default or installed apps can be controlled.

1. Go to the Settings app on your Mobile phone

2. Select the option labeled ⊞ Apps
3. Select an option to edit:
- Select default apps for specific actions: Apps for sending message, browsing the web, making call and more can be selected.
- Settings for Samsung apps: From here you will see the list of Samsung apps and customize their settings as you want.
- Your apps: Select an app to view and update the information about its privacy and usage settings.

TIP: To reset apps preferences, select ⋮ More options, then select Reset apps.

Chapter Five
Contacts

The Contacts app is an app where you can create, edit, delete, store and manage contacts on your device.

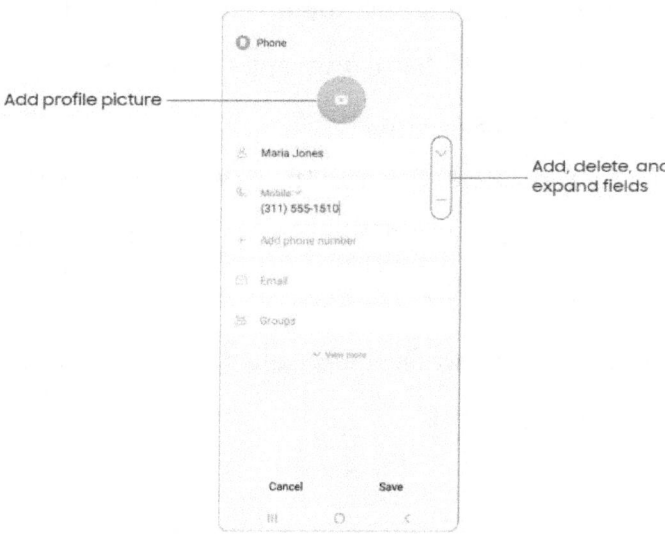

Create a contact

1. To create a contact, go to the Apps screen and select ⊙ Contacts
2. Select ＋ Create contact.
3. Enter the info for the contact you want to create.

4. Select Save.

Edit a contact

1. To edit a contact on the ● Contacts app, select the contact.
2. Select the ✎ Edit option.
3. Choose any field to change or maybe delete information.
4. When you are done select Save.

Favorites

Favorite contacts can be easily accessed from the Contacts list as they are grouped on top of your contact list.

1. Unlock your device and swipe upward from the Home screen to access the Apps screen then select the ● Contacts app icon.
2. Select a contact and tap the ☆ Favorites icon to mark it as a favorite.
- The contact can also be removed from your favorite list when you tap ★ Favorites.

Share a contact

1. To share you contacts with your friends and family members, you first have to unlock your device and swipe upward from the Home screen to display the Apps and select the 👤 Contacts app, then choose a contact to share.
2. Select the 🔗 share icon on the number you want to share.
3. You can decide to share it as a File or Text.
4. Then, choose the method you want to use in sharing the contacts and follow the instructions.

TIP: To Quickly share a contact information with friends while viewing it, select ⋮ More options and touch the QR code scanner.

Groups

Assemble contact using group.

Create a group

1. To create a group and organize your contacts, unlock your mobile phone and go the Apps screen by swiping upward from the Home screen, then choose ⊙ Contacts app and click on the ≡ Open drawer icon then Groups.
2. You can create a new group by pressing Create group option.
3. Select a field below to enter the group information:
- Name of the new Group: Assign a name o to your group for easy location on the Contacts app.
- Ringtone for the group: Create a ringtone for the group.
- Upload members to the group you created: Select contacts to be added to the new group.
- Select done after doing the processes
4. Select the option "Save" to save the changes.

Add or remove group contacts

- o Launch 👤 Contacts application, select ≡ > Groups, and then touch a group to add or remove group members.
- Contacts can be removed from a group by simply pressing and holding the contact to select it then tap 🗑 Remove icon.
- Select the contact you want to add to the group after clicking the ✎ Edit icon and tapping Add member.
- When you are done with the editing adding or removing contact from the group select Done and then click Save.

Send a message to a group

1. To send a message to all members of a group at a time, you have to first unlock your mobile phone and swipe upward from the Home screen to reveal the Apps screen, tap the 👤 Contacts application, tap ≡ and then select "Groups".

2. To send the message select ⋮ More options and choose the option "Send message"

Send an email to a group

1. The first step to take in sending an email to a group is to unlock your Smartphone and go straight to the 👤 Contacts app, touch ≡ > Groups and then select a group.

2. To send the email select ⋮ More options and tap Send email.

3. Select contacts and click Done

- This message will only be visible to group members that have email address attached to their profile.

4. Choose an email account and follow the onscreen prompts.

Delete a group

1. The first step to take towards creating a group is opening the device default 👤 Contacts app, then clicking on the ≡ Open drawer

menu and Groups, and select a group to be deleted.

2. After choosing the group, select ⋮ More options then Delete.

- To remove the group alone, select Delete group only
- To remove both the group and the members in it, select Delete group and members.

Merge contacts

1. To merge multiple contact with the same identity into one entry, go to the 😊 Contacts app either on your Home screen or the Apps screen, then click ☰ Open drawer > Manage contacts.

2. Click Merge contacts. Contacts with identical names, phone numbers, and email addresses will be listed as one.

3. Click the contacts to pick them, and touch Merge.

Delete duplicate contacts

Contacts with duplicate identity can be deleted from your device.

1. From the device Apps screen launch the 👤 Contacts app, then choose the option ≡ Open drawer > Manage contacts.
2. Select the Delete Duplicate Contacts option. You will see the list of comparable contacts.
3. Select the contacts you want to delete, and tap the Delete option.

Import contacts

1. To import contacts to your Smartphone as a vCard file (VCF), go straight to the Home screen and swipe upward to reveal the Apps screen the choose the option 👤 Contacts, then click icon ≡ Open drawer > Manage contacts.
2. Select the "Import" or "Export" contact.
3. Select "Import" from the menu and follow the easy steps.

Export contacts

You can export contacts from your phone as vCard files (VCF).

1. To export contacts from your Smartphone as a vCard file, head straight to the Home screen and swipe the Screen upward to launch the 👤 Contacts app from the Apps screen, then in the contact app select ☰ Open drawer > Manage contacts.
2. Select the option "Import" or "Export".
3. Select "Export" from the menu and follow the easy steps that will show on the screen.

Sync contacts

1. Keeping contacts up to date in all your account across all device that are signed in to you account is easy, just simply launch the 👤 Contacts app, then choose the option ☰ Open drawer > Manage contacts.
2. Choose the option "Sync contacts".

Delete contacts

Do the following to delete multiple or a single contact.

1. From your Smartphone multiple contacts or a single contact can be deleted within a twinkle of an eye, all you need do is, go directly in the ![icon] Contacts app, either from the Home or Apps screen, then press and hold a contact to choose it for deletion.
2. To delete the selected contact (s), follow the easy steps that will appear after selecting ![trash icon] Delete.

Chapter Six
Internet

Use Samsung Internet app for better browsing experience because it is fast, secure, and reliable. You can also experience a safe browsing experience with Secret Mode, Biometric Web Login and Content Blocker.

Browser tabs

Using the browser tabs, multiple websites can be view at the same time.

- To open a new tab on your mobile phone, launch the 🌐 Internet software, then click New tab under the 1️⃣ Tabs option

- To clock the tabs, still go to the 1 Tabs menu and click ⊗ Close tab

Create a Bookmark

  o To create Bookmarks for frequently used apps for easy access, unlock your Smartphone and access the ◯ Internet app from either the Home or Apps screen, click icon ☆ Add to bookmarks to save the launch webpage.

Open a Bookmark

1. To launch the Bookmarked page from the ◯ Internet app, click ☆ Bookmarks.
2. Select from your list of bookmarked pages.

Save a web page

  o To save a webpage there are few option in the ◯ Internet app, but to see these options you have to click on ☰ Tools >Add page, then the options will appear:
- Bookmarks: From the internet app you can Bookmark your Favorite webpage.

- Quick access: You can view of the list of web pages that you access almost all the time from the Internet app.
- Home screen: From the internet app you can create a webpage shortcut that will appear on the Home screen.
- Saved pages: From the internet app you can save webpage content to your Smartphone so it can be viewed offline.

View history

o Your browsing history from your Internet app can be seen when you select ☰ Tools in the ◯ Internet app.

TIP: Select ⋮ More options then clear history to remove your browsing history.

Share pages

You can share your web pages with your contacts.

o To share web pages with your family, friend and on other social media platforms, simply go to the ◯ Internet application and select the ☰ Tools icon then Share, and follow the easy steps.

Secret mode

There will be no traces of pages viewed in secret mode as they are not displayed in your search history or browser history. The secret is also darker than the normal tab when browsing.

After you leave the secret mode menu, files you have downloaded will still be available on your device.

1. To utilize the Secret mode, launch the ⊙ Internet app, then select [1] Tabs menu and then touch Turn on secret mode.
2. To initiate the secret mode browsing, select Start.

Secret mode settings

To run the secret mode feature effectively, a password or a biometric lock is required

1. To set this up, unlock your mobile device and go to the ⊙ Internet app, then click [1] Tabs.
2. The following option will be accessible when you tap the ⋮ More options button and click Secret mode settings:

- Utilize password: Create a password for secret mode, a very strong one at that.

- Face: To privatize your secret mode, you can enable the Face recognition process

- Fingerprints: To privatize your secret mode, you can set up a fingerprint.

- Secret mode reset: From here, your secret mode data can be cleared and your secret mode restored to default settings.

Turn off secret mode

To disable secret mode and go to the normal browsing mode from the Internet app do the following

- Launch the ⊙ Internet app, then click 🔲 Tabs and tap Switch off secret mode thereafter.

Messages

From this app called "Messages" you can quickly say hello to friends and families, start up a conversation make calls, block numbers and also share photos.

- To access the 💬 Messages app on your mobile phone, unlock your device and swipe upward from the Home screen to reveal the Apps screen if the Messages icon is not on the Home screen, then click it icon and select 💬 Compose to create a new message.

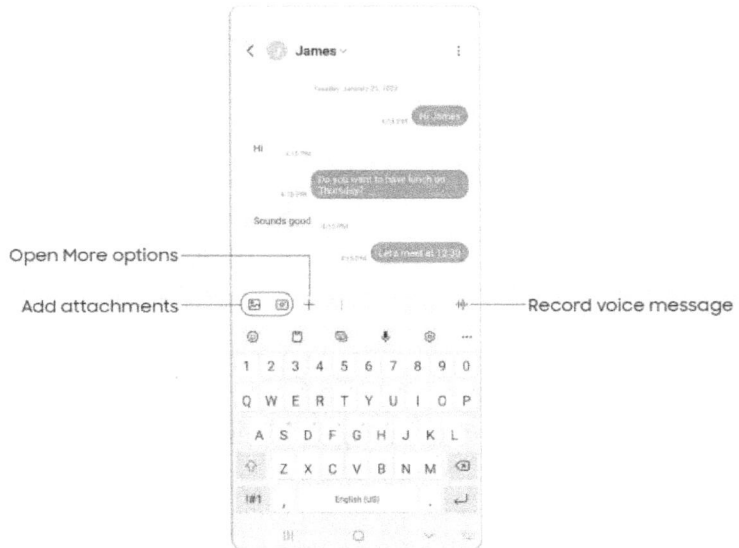

Message search

The search feature on the Messages app can enable you look for messages that you are unsure of where to find them.

1. After entering the 💬 Messages app on your Smartphone, you will see the 🔍 Search icon, click on it.
2. Enter the word (s) to search for and select 🔍 Search.

Delete conversations

Conversations will be removed from history once they are deleted.

1. Select the ⋮ More option button on the 💬 Messages app screen and select Delete.
2. Select the messages that are to be deleted.
3. Follow the onscreen instructions that will appear after you press 🗑 Delete all to delete the messages.

Send SOS messages

When you are in a pressing situation, don't bother, because this feature helps you to call for help in an emergency situation by sending messages of your location to emergency numbers.

1. Tap the ⬤ Advances features button and click on Send SOS message and tap ⬤ On to activate this setting from the Settings app.

   - Select either 3 or 4 times press on the Side key for the SOS message to be sent.
   - Select Auto call someone to select a contact to call after sending an SOS message.
   - Choose Attach image, so you can add images from your front or rear camera.
   - To send a 5 seconds audio recording alongside your messages, select Attach audio recording.
   - To add a new contact or pick from your phone contacts, select Send message.

2. To send the message, press the side key for about three to four times.

Message settings

To set up messages or edit the messages settings for multimedia messages do the following.

o From 💬 Messages click the ⋮ More option Button and select settings to confiogure message settings.

Emergency alerts

With this feature activated on your mobile device you will be alerted of threats that are coming to your device. No charges are applied to receiving an emergency message.

1. To activate this, select Advanced settings under 💬Notification under the Settings menu.
2. To change the emergency alert notification, select Wireless Emergency Alerts.

My Files

The My Files app on your Mobile phone can make you access all file like the photos, videos, music and more that are stored on your phone. From this app, you will be able to view and control all files stored on your SD card or cloud accounts.

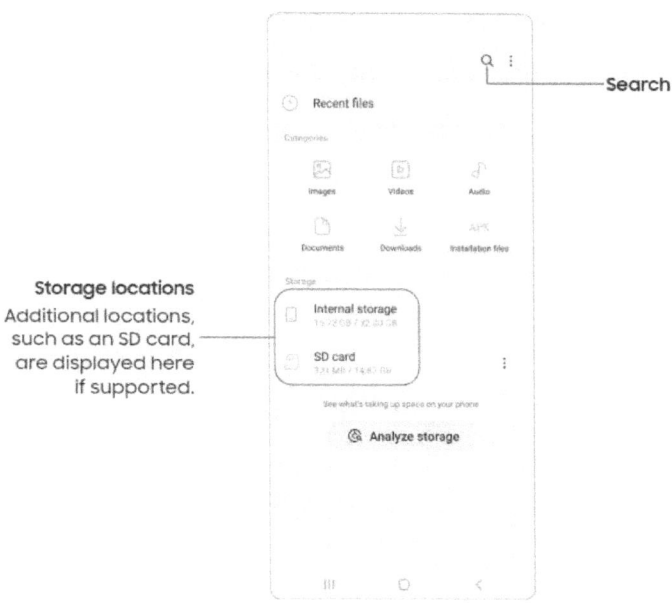

File groups

To get files stored on your device, access the following groups:

- Recent files: From here, all files that you have opened recently will be seen.

- Categories: From here, files can be viewed based on their type.
- Storage: From here, the files that are stored on your phone storage, Cloud accounts and SD card can be viewed.
  - Depending on the service you sign in to, Cloud accounts varies.
- Storage analysis: From here, you can analyze your storage and see what is taking up your space.

My Files options

More things like, editing, removing the file history, searching for files can be done use the My Files options.

- o Enter the ⬜ My Files app for the following options:
- 🔍 Search: Use this feature to look for a file or a folder.
- ⋮ More settings:
  - Cloud service: Connect to a cloud service on your mobile device.

- Analyze storage: Analyze your storage to see what's eating up your space.

- Trash: Once any file is taken from trash, the file will be deleted from your mobile device permanently.

- Settings: From here, you can view the settings of the app.

Chapter Seven
Phone

Calls can be made, received, declined and sent to voicemail in the Phone app. From the Phone app you can also view favorite contacts and recent calls.

Calls

From any screen page, calls can be made, answered, declined with the Phone app.

Make a call

To makes a call do the following while on the Phone.

- Enter the keypad and enter the number you want to call from the Phone app and tap Call.

Make a call from Recent

Calls can be made from your list of recent calls.

- Select the number you want to call from your recent call list in the Phone app then select the Call option.

Make a call from Contacts

Calls can be made from the Contacts app on your Smartphone by taking the following action.

- Swipe your finger to the right across the contact you want to call to call it from the Contacts app.

Answer a call

Your phone will ring and the caller ID will appear on the incoming call screen when the call comes in.

- You have the choice to answer an incoming call on the incoming call screen just by dragging the

Answer button to the right side of the screen.

Decline a call

- You have the choice to also reject the call that comes in and send it to voicemail just by dragging the Reject button to the left side of the screen.

Decline with a message

Text messages can be used to decline an incoming call when you are busy or not in the right position to answer the call, take the action highlighted below to decline a call with a message.

- Drag the Send message option upward and choose a message to send to the person.

End a call

When you are done making a call you can decide to end it. Take the action highlighted below to end an ongoing call.

- Select the End button on the ongoing call screen.

Actions while on a call

A call can be ongoing, and you are still performing other task on that same device, tasks like increasing and decreasing the volume, switching from your device speaker to a Bluetooth headset. To increase or decrease the call volume, take that action that is highlighted below:

- o Press either of the Volume keys (Up to increase the volume or Down to decrease the volume).

Switch to headset or speaker

On this device you are currently using you can answer call via external hearing device like the Bluetooth headset. To answer a call through an external device like the Bluetooth headset or the device's main speaker, take this step that is shown below.

- o Touch the 🔊 Speaker button to listen to the caller using the speaker or touch ✶ Bluetooth button to listen to the caller using a Bluetooth headset.

Multitask

Leaving the screen of the ongoing call to use another program on your device will cause the active call to appear on the status bar of the phone.

Take the below step to return to the call screen:

- o Drag the Status bar downward and touch the call.

Take the step that is shown below to end a call while multitasking:

- o Select the End call button after dragging the Status bar downward to display the active call.

Call background

While on an active call, select the background to appear. To do this take the following steps highlighted below

- o Unlock your device and swipe upward from the bottom of the Home screen to reveal the Apps screen then select the Phone app icon, then click More options > Settings > Call background:

- Layout: If the caller has a profile picture attached to his/her contact, select how the caller info will display.
- Background: A background can be chosen from your pictures to apps during a call.

Call pop-up settings

While other programs (applications) are in use, any call coming in will appear as a pop-up window.

- o Access the Home screen menu and launch the Phone app, then select the More options button> Settings > Call display while using applications.
- Full screen: From here, calls can be set to appear on a full screen view when they come in.
- Pop-up: From here, calls can be set to appear a pop-up window on top of your screen.
- Mini pop-up: From here, calls can be set to appear as a smaller pop-up when they come in.
- Keep calls in pop-up: Calls that are answered will remain in the pop-up window when this function is activated.

Manage calls

From the call logs where all your calls recorded you can manage the actions of calls, block numbers, set speed dials and also set up voicemail.

Call log

This is a location where all your calls are recorded, whether, missed, answered or dialed.

- To access the Call log, go to the 🅒 Phone app then click "Recent" to see the full list of recently made calls. The name of the caller will appear on the call log if the number is not in your contact list.

Save a contact from a recent call

Call that made can be saved from your recent calls where they are recorded.

1. Select the "Recent" option in the 🅒 Phone app.
2. From the list of calls, select the one that has the details you want to add to your contact list then click "Add to contact".
3. After tapping the contact, select "Create new contact" or "Update existing contacts".

Delete call records

To clear your entire call log or delete a single contact from the call log, take the following actions below:

1. Select the option labeled "Recent" in the 🅒 Phone app menu.
2. Look for the call you want to delete, and then press and hold it.
3. Select the icon 🗑 Delete to confirm your deletion.

Block a number

After blocking a number, you will not receive a call from the contact, messages will not also be received as well, when they try to call, the call will be declined and sent to voicemail.

1. Select the "Recent" option under the 🅒 Phone menu.
2. Choose the contact you need to block.
3. After seeing the number, click 🛈 Details > 🚫 Block, and confirm the action.

TIP: From the 🌀 Phone, click ⋮ More options> Settings > Block numbers to also block a contact.

Speed dial

To assign a shortcut (speed dial) number to a contact, take the following actions.

1. To set a speed dial number, launch the 🌀 Phone app, then click Keypad and then ⋮ More options, and finally select Speed dial numbers. All the speed dial numbers that are reserved will appear on the speed dial screen.
2. Select a number that has not been assigned to a contact.
   - To select another number apart from the ones that are listed in the sequence select the ▼ Menu icon.
   - The "1" number is always reserved for voicemail.
3. To assign number to a contact, enter the contact or click 👤 Add from Contacts.
   - Contacts you have selected will appear in the box of speed dial.

Make a call with Speed dial

Calls can be made by entering speed dial numbers.

- o To make a call with speed dial, launch the ⓒ Phone application, then press and hold the Speed dial number.
- • If your speed dial number is longer than a digit, all you need do is enter the first digit of the speed dial number then press and hold the last digit.

Remove a Speed dial number

To remove a number that has been assigned to a contact, take the following procedures.

1. Select "Speed dial" under the menu of ⁞More options in the ⓒ Phone app.
2. Next to the contact you will see the delete icon, click it ▬ to remove the speed dial number.

Emergency calls

With an inactivated device, emergency call can be made.

1. To make emergency call, first go to the 🅒 Phone app, then enter the emergency number for your regions and select Call.

TIP: While your screen is locked emergency numbers can still be dialed.

Phone settings

All settings that are associated with your Phone app can be customized form the Phone settings.

o To change the Phone app settings, launch the 🅒 Phone app from the home or Apps screen, then select ⋮More options.

Optional calling services

The calling services that are listed below might be supported by your device wireless carrier and service plan.

Place a multi-party call

You can make a conference call from this menu.

1. To start a second call while a call is ongoing, select the ＋ Add call icon.
2. After answering the second call:

- Select ⟲ Swap to change between the call you want to answer.
- Touch ⤳ Merge to hear the two callers at the same time.

Video calls

Start a video call:

- To initiate a video, call on your device, launch the ⓒ Phone application then select the video calls options ▣ or ▣ or ◯.

Real Time Text (RTT)

When a device supports the RTT calling feature or if it is connected to a teletypewriter (TTY), you can use the RTT calling feature to call it. If and RTT call comes in, you will see the RTT icon.

1. Go to the Setting menu under the ⋮More option in the 🅒 Phone app.
2. Select "Real Time Text"

- RTT call button: Choose are the RTT call button should appear.
- Make us of an external TTY keyboard: The RTT keyboard can be hidden if an external one is connected to your device.
- TTY mode: Choose TTY mode for the keyboard that you are currently using.

Samsung Health

With the Samsung Health application, you can monitor your day to day activities such as your diet and exercise routine and more. Visit samsung.com/us/support/owners/app/samsung-health to download more information about this app.

TIP: Samsung Health or other related apps is not intended to use the information collected from this device for the diagnosis of disease or infections, or curing them, mitigation and treating them.

The facts provided by the device may be affected by factors such as environmental conditions, user configuration or user provided details and more.

Before you start exercising

Your heath physician or medical practitioner must be consulted before you start an exercise routine if you have any of the conditions listed below. For most people it is safe to do an activity such as brisk walking.

- Heart disease, Lung disease, Diabetes, liver or kidney disease and Arthritis.

- Chest Pain, neck pain, pain in the arm region during activities;
- Consciousness Loss;
- Swelling ankle, mostly in the night;
- Unusual heartbeat;

Settings
Access Settings

The Phone settings can be accessed in so many ways on your device.

- To access Settings from the Home screen, swipe downward to display the notification panel and select the ⚙ Settings button.
- To access Settings from the Apps screen, select the 🅾 Settings button.

Search for Settings

Settings can be found and seen on your device when you use the search feature.

1. To search for the apps or settings, launch the Settings app and click the 🔍 Search button.
2. Select a result to launch the setting.

Chapter Eight
Connections

Connections between your device and other mobile networks can be monitored and managed.

Wi-Fi

You can connect to a friend's Hotspot or a public inter connection if you have Wi-Fi turned on.

1. Swipe upward from the Home screen to show the Apps screen then select the Setting app and click 📶 Connections > Wi-Fi, after tapping the Connections then Wi-Fi press the ⚪On icon to scan for available networks.

2. Select a network to connect to and enter it password if the connection is locked.

Connect to a hidden Wi-Fi network

If the network you want to connect is still not listed after a network scan, you will have to input the hotspot connection details (Name, password and security type).

1. From your Home screen you can access the Settings app, but if it is not found there, just

swipe upward to the Apps screen and choose the option "Settings" then click 🛜 Connections > Wi-Fi, after select Connection and clicking Wi-Fi press 🌑 On to activate the Wi-Fi.

2. Select the ➕ Add option that is displayed at the bottom part of the network list.
3. Input the network details:
- Network name: Enter the network precise name.
- Security: Select an option for it security and enter the password if required.
- Advanced: IP and Proxy options.
4. When you are done, select Save.

TIP: You can connect to the Network connection by using your Phone to scan the QR code, select 🔳 QR scanner icon.

Advanced Wi-Fi settings

From the advanced Wi-Fi settings menu, you can sort connection or different kind and from different source, manage saved networks and search your phone network address.

1. If you cannot access the Setting page on the Home screen, swipe upward from the Home screen to access the Apps screen and launch the app the click 🛜 Connections > Wi-Fi, and then touch ⬤ On to switch on Wi-Fi.

2. Select Advanced under ⋮ More options.

- Alternate to mobile data: After this feature has be successfully activated, your mobile phone will switch to mobile data automatically if the network connection is not steady, then switches back to the Wi-Fi again if the Wi-Fi signal is strong enough.

- Automatically put Wi-Fi on: Your device can be set to enable Wi-Fi while you are in location that you have used Wi-Fi frequently.

- Network notifications: Once your device detects open networks in range you will get a notification.

- Network management: From, here saved networks can be reconnected to or forgotten.
- Wi-Fi control history: From here, apps that have used your Wi-Fi recently will appear.
- Hotspot 2.0: Your device can be set to connect to a Hotspot that supports Hotspot 2.0.
- Install authentication certificates.

Wi-Fi Direct

With this feature connections can be share between devices directly.

1. Go to Settings apps, select Connection, tap Wi-Fi and tap On to turn the Wi-Fi on.
2. Select Wi-Fi direct under ⋮More options.
3. Choose a device to connect, and follow the onscreen instructions.

Disconnect from Wi-Fi Direct

To leave a Wi-Fi direct connection, take the following actions.

- o Access the Settings app either on your Home screen or Apps screen then tap Connection and select Wi-Fi then ⋮More options and lastly tap Wi-Fi Direct. Choose a device to disconnect it.

Bluetooth

With your mobile phone connected to a Bluetooth device, you can share files like Pictures, video, Music and documents. Turn on your Bluetooth so that your device can pair with device like headphones and vehicle infotainment system.

1. Access the settings app either on the Home screen or the Apps screen, select 📶 Connections and then tap Bluetooth and select ⬤ On to activate the Bluetooth.
2. Choose a device to connect to and follow the easy steps.

Rename a paired device

Give a device your own name for easy recognition.

1. To rename a paired device, enter the Settings app, choose 📶 Connection and then Select Bluetooth and tap ⬤.

2. To change the name of the device, next to it you will see an icon ⚙ Settings, click it.
3. Enter the name you want to give to the device and select Rename.

Un-pair from a Bluetooth device

Once a connection is broken between two devices, you will need to pair tem together again to get them connected.

1. To un-pair from a Bluetooth device, first tap ⬤ to turn on Bluetooth under Bluetooth in the 📶 Connections menu from the Settings app.
2. Next to the device name, you will see a ⚙ Settings icon click it.

Advanced options

Go to the advanced menu to access the following Bluetooth features.

1. From your Galaxy A15 device, go to the Settings app, click 📶 Connections and then tap Bluetooth.

2. Select ⋮ More options and tap Advanced features:
- Link files with Samsung Cloud: With your Samsung account, you can sync files that are transferred via Bluetooth.
- Music Share: Use this feature to share music with friends and families on social media platforms.
- Ringtone sync: Set a ringtone to use on your phone when calls are received through a Bluetooth device that is connected.
- Bluetooth control history: From here, applications that have used Bluetooth recently will appear.
- Block pairing requests: Add device you don't want to accept their pairing request here.

NFC and payment

You can use this feature to commune with other without requiring any network connection. You can only use this feature with device that supports it and the device must be about 4cm away from your device.

- o To access this from the Settings application, select 🛜 Connection and click NFC and contactless payment then tap ⬤.

Tap and pay

Place the back of your device to a compatible card reader to make payments to application with the NFC payment application.

1. To do this from the Settings app, select 🛜 Connections and then tap NFC and contactless payments, and then click ⬤.
2. To open the default payment app, select Contactless payment.
- Select an app available for use, so you can use it as your payment app.

- Select Pay with currently open app to make the payment through another app that is open.
- Select other, to use another payment service as default, and then select the service you want.

Airplane mode

To automatically turn off all connectivity like the Bluetooth, Calling, Texting, Wi-Fi, Data, Hotspot, just turn on the Airplane mode (Flight mode).

- o To turn it on from Settings, click on 📶 Connections, tap Airplane mode, and then click ⊙.

TIP: The rules governing Aircrafts and Ship may be against the use of smartphone while on a trip.

Mobile networks

The new Galaxy A15 has the ability to connect a mobile network and use mobile data.

- o Launch Settings from the Application screen, scroll down and tap 📶 Connections > Mobile networks.
- Mobile data: Permit the use of mobile data.

- International data roaming: For international roaming, you can change the text, voice and data roaming.
- Allow 2G service: In areas with limited cellular coverage, you can use the 2G service.
- Access Point Names: Choose APNs (Access Point Names). It has the network settings your phone needs to connect to your provider.
- Network operators: Choose from the list of available networks.

Data usage

Your data usage and Wi-Fi usage can be monitored. Limitations can also be set.

- From the Galaxy A15 Home or Apps screen, tap Settings, click 📶 Connections and lastly press Data usage.

Turn on Data saver

Reduction of your data consumption can be done easily be done by turning n the Data saver mode which also prevent running apps in background form sending data.

1. Press and hold the 📶 Connections in the settings app, select Data usage and tap Data saver.
2. To turn on Data saver, tap ⬤.

- Some applications can be allowed to use data without restrictions, just tap allowed to make use of data while Data saver is activated then touch ⬤ next to each app.

Monitor mobile data

Set limit to manage and monitor your mobile data.

- o From your Home or Apps screen, open the Settings app, tap Connections and then Data usage.
  - Mobile data: Set your device to make use of data from your monthly plan.
  - International data roaming: While roaming internationally, you can turn on mobile data services.
  - Mobile data only apps: Some apps can be set to use mobile data even when your device is connection to a Wi-Fi network.
  - Mobile data usage: Look at the data usage over time.
  - Billing cycle and data warning: To align your monthly plan with your carrier's billing data, you need to change it.

NOTE: Using this feature can enable you to monitor the actual data usage.

Monitor Wi-Fi data

1. To monitor Wi-Fi data and set limits, go to the Settings app on your Home or Apps screen, select Connections and then tap Data usage.
2. To view the usage of data over time, click Wi-Fi data usage.

Mobile hotspot

To share your mobile phone data or internet connection with other devices, turn on your mobile hotspot.

1. Tap Settings application, press Connection > Mobile Hotspot & Tethering > Mobile Hotspot and then press the activation button to turn on Hotspot.
2. Tell the person operating the other device to turn on their Wi-Fi, look for your device and enter the password to connect.

TIP: Connections can be made easily when you scan your device's QR code, just tap QR code.

Configure mobile hotspot settings

1. To configure your mobile hotspot connection settings, go to the Settings app and select Connections > click Mobile hotspot & Tethering > Mobile hotspot.
2. Select "Configure" for the following to appear:

- Network name: View your Hotspot name and change edit or change it.
- Security: Choose the level of security your mobile hotspot uses.
- Password: View the password that you are currently using and set a strong one.
- Band: Select from the list of available bandwidth options.
- Advanced: More Hotspot settings can be customized form here.

Auto hotspot

1. To share your mobile hotspot with device that are signed into your Samsung account automatically, launch the Settings application from either the Home or Apps screen the select

Connections > Mobile hotspot & Tethering > Mobile hotspot.

2. Select to turn on Auto Hotspot.

Tethering

1. To share your device internet with a computer via a USB cable, simply go straight to the Settings app, select Connections > touch Mobile hotspot & Tethering.
2. Choose from the options below:
- Select USB tethering to connect to the computer via a USB cable.
- Select Ethernet tethering to connect to the computer via an Ethernet adapter.

Connect to a printer

1. To connect your mobile phone to a printer for easy printing of file, launch the Settings app and select Connections > More connection settings > Printing.
2. Select the Default print service options, click More options and then tap Add printer.

- Select "Download plug-in" and follow the easy steps to add a print service if your computer needs a plug-in.

TIP: Printing is not supported by all application.

Virtual Private Networks

1. To connect to a private network with your mobile phone via VPN, request for connection info from your VPN administrator.

   NOTE: The VPN stands for Virtual Private Networks

2. From the Home screen, launch the Settings app, select 🛜 Connections > More connection settings and then tap VPN.

3. Select Add VPN profile under ⋮ More options

4. Enter the info of the VPN network provided to you by your network administrator.

5. Select "Save" when you are done.

Manage a VPN

1. To manage a VPN, launch the Settings app, select 🛜 Connections > More connection settings" options > VPN.

2. Next to the VPN you will see a ⚙ Setting icon select it.
3. Edit the VPN to your taste and tap "Save"
4. Click "Delete" to remove the VPN.

Connect to a VPN

Follow the procedure under to join a Virtual Private Network.

1. To connect to a VPN on your device, launch your phone's Settings app and select 📶 Connections.
2. Select the "More connection settings" option > VPN.
3. Select the Virtual Private Network you want to connect to and select "Connect".
- Simply click the VPN you want to disconnect from and tap "Disconnect" to disconnect from a network.

Private DNS

Follow the steps below to configure your phone to connect to a private DNS.

1. To configure your mobile device to connect to a private DNS host, launch the Settings app and click 📶 Connections.
2. Select "More connection settings" > Private DNS.
3. To set up a Private DNS connection, select any of the available options.
4. Select Save.

Ethernet

1. When wireless network connection is not available, connect an Ethernet adapter to your phone to join a local network.
2. Launch the Settings app and click the 📶 Connections option.
3. Select the "More connection settings" options then Ethernet, and follow the on-screen instruction.

Sounds and vibration

Manage all sounds and vibration that are used to indicate notifications, calls and other sounds.

Sound mode

- o To select a sound mode that fits your hearing, go to the Settings application and choose a mode under 🔊 Sounds & vibration:
- • Sound: For notifications and alerts, you can use the sound vibrations, and volume levels you have selected in the Sound settings.
- – Vibrate while ringing: Enable your device to ring with a vibration.
- • Vibrate: Enable your device to use vibration only for alerts and notifications.
- • Mute: Mute your device to avoid disturb
- – Temporary mute: Enable your phone to mute the sound for a certain period of time.

Vibrations

1. To control how and when your phone vibrates, go to the Settings menu and select 🔊 Sounds & vibration.

2. Select an option to customize:
- Call vibration pattern: Choose a call vibration pattern you prefer.
- Notification vibration pattern: Choose a notification vibration pattern you prefer.
- Vibration intensity: Pull the Vibration slider to set vibration intensity for Calls, Taps and notifications.

Volume

o To adjust calls ringtone, media, notification and system sound, volume level, launch the Settings > select 🔊 Sounds & vibration > Volume, and pull the sliders for each sound type.

TIP: The volume keys by the side of device can be used to regulate the volume. A pop-up menu will appear showing the current volume level of your device when you press the side key, move the slider to increase or decrease the volume.

Media volume limit

1. To set a media volume output for your phone using headphones or Bluetooth speaker, launch Settings and select 🔊 Sounds & vibration > Volume.

2. Select Media Volume limit under ⋮ more options.

3. Press ⬤ to make the feature active.

- Use the Custom volume limit slider to set the maximum output you want by dragging it.

- To set a Pin to make change to the volume settings, select "Set Volume Limit PIN".

Ringtone

1. To set a ringtone or add from your local files, enter Settings, tap 🔊 Sounds & vibration > Ringtone.

2. Tap a preloaded ringtone to hear a preview of them before applying it or click ➕ Add to set a ringtone from your local files.

Notification sound

1. To set a notification sound for incoming notifications, launch Settings, tap 🔊 Sounds & vibration and tap Notification sound.
2. Click on a sound to hear a brief play before applying it.

System sounds and vibration

o To set sound and vibration for actions such as touches and charging, go to Settings, click 🔊 Sounds & vibration > System sound/vibration control for the following options:

Sound

- Tap interactions: You can set your mobile device to make a sound when you touch the screen.
- Screens lock/unlock: You can set your mobile device to make a sound when you lock or unlock the device.
- Charging: When a charger is connected, your device will make a sound if you set it to do so.

- Dial pad tones: While dialing on the keypad, your phone will emit a sound when enabled.
- Samsung keyboard: While typing with the Samsung Keyboard, set your phone to make a sound if enabled.

Vibration
- o Enable the following to feel a vibration when they are in use:
- Touch interactions: When navigation buttons are touched, your phone will vibrate.
- Dialing keypad: When dialing on the keypad, your phone will vibrate.
- Navigation gestures: When using gesture, you phone will vibrate.
- Charging: Your device will vibrate while charging.
- Samsung keyboard: Your phone will vibrate when typing on the Samsung keyboard.

Do not disturb

If you don't want to get disturbed with sound from calls and notifications, turn on Do Not Disturb. You can also select apps, notifications and calls you would not like to receive disturbance from.

- o To access the Do Not Disturb options below, open the Settings app from the Home or Apps screen and select ⬤ Notifications >Do not disturb:
- Do not disturb: Once you enable this, you will silent all sounds that are coming from call and notifications.
- For how long?: You can set up a time to manually enable Do not Disturb.

Schedule

- Sleeping: Set a sleeping schedule for Do not Disturb mode
- Add schedule: Set up a routine to set the days for your device to be put in the Do not Disturb mode regularly.

Exceptions

- Calls, messages, and conversations: Tap to set Do not disturb exceptions permission
- Alarms and sounds: While this mode is on, turn on sounds and vibrations for alarms, events, reminders and more
- Apps: From here, add apps that you want to get notifications from in Do not Disturb mode
- Don't show notifications: You can check editing options that enables you hide notifications.

Alert when phone picked up

Setting this you will get notified about missed calls and messages from your phone by vibrating when you pick it up

- Go to the Settings menu and select the Advanced features option>Motions and gestures >Alert.

Turn over to mute

Turn your device to face the ground to mute incoming calls, alarms and messages.

- Enter the Apps screen and select Settings then Click ⚙ Advanced features> Motions and gestures >Flip to mute, and touch ⬤.

Chapter Nine
Display

Configure the device screen brightness, font size, timeout delay and many other display settings.

Dark mode

Enable "Dark mode" to help you look at your phone more comfortably at night and avoid eye damage.

- o To access the display options below, launch the Settings app on your Apps screen or Home screen and tap ⚙ Display:
- Light: The light theme is the default them for your phone.
- Dark: The dark color theme can be applied to your mobile device.
- Dark mode settings: Set up a routine for when and where dark mode is to be applied.
- – Turn on as scheduled: You can schedule dark mode to turn on either in Sunrise or Sunset.
- – Adaptive color filter: This feature allows you to look at your device more comfortably at night and reduce the dame of the eyes. Turn on Blue

light filter between sunset and sunrise automatically.

Screen brightness

Adjust the brightness of your screen to fit your eyes.

1. Enter ⚙ Display under the Settings of your Smartphone.
2. The following options are customizable:
- Adjust the brightness with the provided slider.
- To adjust the screen illumination based on the conditions of light around you select Adaptive brightness.

TIP: While on the Quick Setting panel, the brightness level can still be adjusted.

Motion smoothness

You can taste the smoothness of scrolling and more realistic animation by increasing the refresh rate of the screen.

1. Select Motion Smoothness in the Settings app while in the ⚙ Display menu.
2. Select an option and click Apply.

Eye comfort shield

You can use your Smartphone comfortably at night when you turn on this feature. You can set a routine to turn on and off this feature automatically.

- o Unlock your phone and enter the settings app to access the ☼ Display menu then tap Eye comfort shield, and then select an option:
  - Select "Set schedule", depending on your usage habit you can select "Always on" "Sunrise" "Sunset" or "Custom".
  - Drag the slider for temperature to adjust the filter opacity.

Font size and style

The typing fonts of your Samsung phone can be changed.

- o Select "Font size and style" in the ☼ Display menu under settings to access the following:
  - To apply a different font, select Font style.
  - Choose a font or Click ➕ to download from the Galaxy Store.

- All text will apply in bold weights when you tap "Bold font".
- Size of the font will be change when you drag the Font size slider.

Screen zoom

To make content easier to see on your phone change the level of the zoom. Do the following to change the zoom level.

1. Start with the Settings app opening then tapping ⚙ Display icon> Screen zoom.
2. Drag the slider till it fits your choice.

Full screen apps

o To select app that will appear in the full screen view, start by opening Settings then touching ⚙ Display > Full screen apps and click apps to activate this feature.

Screen timeout

With this you can allow your screen to turn off after a set amount of time. it might be 30 seconds or 15 as the case may be.

o Launch the Settings app to start then go to Display icon>Screen timeout, and select a time limit to set it.

Touch sensitivity

Increase the sensitivity of touch to enable your screen respond to taps quickly, when you are using a screen protector.

o Launch the Settings app to begin and touch Display icon then Touch sensitivity to activate it.

Screen saver

Choose a photo or color to beautify your screen with, these colors or photos will appear when your screen is off or when the device is charging.

1. Go to the Settings app to start, then touch the Display option and tap Screen saver.
2. Select from the following options:
- None: Choose not to show a screen saver.
- Colors: Choose the selector to display a changing screen of colors.
- Photo table: Display images in the Photo table.

- Photo frame: Display images in the Photo frame.
- Photos: Configure how photos will appear on your Google Photos account.
3. To view the selected image before applying it to the screen, select "Preview".

TIP: Next to a feature you will see the ⚙ Settings icon, click it to access more options.

Lift to wake

Activate this feature for your device to turn on when you raise it up.

- o Go to the Settings app to start then click ⚙ Advanced features then select Motions and gestures >Lift to wake.

Double tap to turn on screen

Activate this feature so that you can turn on your screen by double tapping it without pressing the Side key.

- o Go to the Settings app to start then click ⚙ Advanced features >Motions and gestures > Double tap to turn on screen.

Double tap to turn off screen

Activate this feature so that you can turn off your device by double tapping the screen without pressing the Side key.

- o Launch the Settings app to start the click ⊕ Advanced features > Motions and gestures > Double tap to turn off screen

Keep screen on while viewing

- o To keep your screen on while you are viewing contents, go to Settings app, click ⊕ Advanced features>Motions and gestures>Keep screen on while viewing, and click ⬤.

One-handed mode

Activate this feature so that you can operate you device with one hand.

1. Go to the Settings menu to get started, then tap ⊕ Advanced features>One-handed mode.
2. Select from the following options after touching ⬤ to activate the feature:

- Gesture: To use Gesture, Swipe down in the middle of the bottom edge of the screen.

- Button: To use the buttons Double tap ⬜ Home in quick succession to reduce the display size.

Lock screen and security

Set a screen lock for your Smartphone's feature to be secured privately.

Screen lock types

The main screen lock type in a phone are, PIN, Patter, Password, Swipe, None, Fingerprint recognition and the Face recognition depending on the model.

Set a secure screen lock

Lock your Phone with a "PIN" "Pattern" "Password" or "Biometric lock" to secure your contents. These lock methods are important when setting up your device.

1. To get started, launch the Settings application and tap 🔒 Lock screen > Screen lock type and

choose the one you prefer (Pattern, PIN, or Password).

2. To enable showing notifications on the lock screen select ⬤. The following options will appear:

- Only Icons: You can set your device to show notification icons without giving you any information about the notification.

- Information: You can also set your device to show notification details on the Lock screen.

- Secrete content of notification: Set your phone not to show notifications in the Notification panel.

- Notifications to show: Select notification that you want to appear on the Lock screen.

3. To exit the menu when you are done select "Done".

4. Use the following options to configure the screen lock:

- Smart Lock: When trusted locations are detected, you can set your phone to unlock automatically. To use this feature effectively, you need a secure screen lock.

- Secure lock settings: Your screen lock settings can be customized from here. For effective performance of this feature, you need a secure screen lock.

Clock and information

The following below can be done to set up feature to appear on the Lock screen such as clock, and others useful feature.

- o To get started, launch the Settings app and select 🔒 Lock screen for the following options:
- Wallpaper services: Turn on more features like the Guide page and Dynamic lock screen.
- Clock style: YO can customize your clock the way you want it.
- Roaming clock: While roaming, set your device to shoe the time.
- Widgets: Personalize Widgets to beautify your home screen ad easy access to certain features.

- Contact info: Personalize your phone to show your contact details, emails address and phone number.

- Notifications: Select the notifications that you want to show on the Lock screen.

- Shortcuts: Select the application shortcuts that you want to apply to the Lock screen.

- About Lock screen: Update your Lock screen software version.

Find My Mobile

Turn on this feature to track a stolen or missing device. With this feature you can also track your device online and remove all the data in it remotely. You need a Samsung account for the operation, and Google location must also be enabled for this feature to work. Visit samsung.com/us/support/owners/app/find-mymobile to learn more.

Turn on Find My Mobile

Enable the Find My Mobile feature in accordance with the following steps

1. To get started, launch the Settings app and select ⭕ Biometrics and security>Find My Mobile.

2. Select the ⬤On icon to enable then sign in to your Samsung account.

3. You will see the following options:

- Unlock Remotely: You can manage your phone in a remote manner by allowing Samsung to save your PIN, Pattern or Password.

- Send last location: Enable the permission for your phone to send the last location the Find My Mobile server if the battery drops under a specific level.

- Find My Mobile update: Check the current version of the software and check for updates.

Find My Device

You Smartphone is protected from loss once this feature is activated. The device can be tacked using the means of internet and the data in it can also be erased remotely. You will need an account of Samsung and Google location must also be turned on of this feature to run effectively.

1. To get started, launch the Settings application of your Phone and enter 🛡 Biometrics and security then tap Find My Device.

- This feature will not work if you are not also signed in to a Google account, login in accordance with the instructions on the screen.

2. The following options are accessible:

- Find My Device: The app can be downloaded from the Google Play Store.
- Web: It can be accessed from the Internet.
- Google: You can go to Google to look for it.

Secure Folder

For other not to access your device and find sensitive content, create a secure folder to protect them. You will also need to sign it to your Samsung Account to create a secure folder.

1. Launch the Settings app to get started and click 🔘 Biometrics and security then tap Secure Folder
2. To create the folder, follow the onscreen instructions.

Private Share

To prevent re-sharing of your content by someone who has access to your device, use the private share to share files.

o Launch the Setting application to get started and tap 🔘 Biometrics and security then select tap Private share and follow the on-screen instruction to add files.

Install unknown apps

Give the device permission to install application from unknown sources.

1. Launch Settings app to begin the click ⬤ Biometrics and security>Install unknown apps.
2. Select an app or source then click allow from this source.

NOTE: Your Smartphone and it personal are exposed to risks by installing apps from unknown sources.

Encrypt or decrypt SD card

Protect the date on your SD card by encrypting it.

1. Enter Settings to get started with the process of encrypting the SD card then tap ⬤ Biometrics and security>Encrypt or decrypt SD card.
2. Select Encrypt SD card
3. Follow the onscreen instruction to code all your SD card data.

TIP: If your SD card is encrypted, it will not be affected by any factory data reset. Make sure that that you decrypt the installed SD card first before starting a factory data reset.

Decrypt SD card

When you want to perform a factory, data reset or use the SD card in another device make sure that your decrypt it first.

1. Go to the Settings to begin the decrypting process then tap ⬤ Biometrics and security > tap Encrypt or decrypt SD card.

2. Tap Decrypt SD card

3. Follow the on-screen instruction to decode all your SD card data.

Password for factory data reset

To reset your phone to factory default, a password is needed.

1. Launch the Setting app to get started then select ⬤ Biometrics and security > Other security settings

2. Select Setup/change password and input a password.

Set up SIM card lock

When your SIM card gets missing or stolen, it cannot be used by another person if your set up a SIM card lock. Options vary by carrier.

1. To get started, launch the Settings application and tap ⭕ Biometrics and security > Other security settings

2. Select Set up SIM card lock and follow the on-screen instruction.

- To turn on this feature, select Lock SIM card, and tap Change SIM card PIN to generate a new PIN.

View passwords

You can set your device to show password as you are typing.

- o Launch Settings to get started and tap ⭕ Biometrics & security > Other security settings > then tap Make passwords visible to turn the feature on.

Device administration

To authorize security features and applications to have administrative access to your Smartphone do the following.

1. Launch the Preference app to begin then tap ⬤ Biometrics and security > Other security settings > then select Device admin apps.
2. Select an option to activate as a device administrator.

Credential storage

The trusted security certificates installed on your Smartphone can be managed.

- o Launch the Preferences to begin the process then tap ⬤ Biometrics and security > Other security settings for the following options:
- Storage type: Select a storage category for your storage type.
- View security certificates: While on your phone's ROM or other certificates that you have installed, you can set your phone to show certificates.

- User certificates: View user certificates that verify your phone.
- Install from device/phone storage: Install a new certificate from your storage.
  - Clear credentials: From here, clear credential contents from the phone and reset the password.

Permission manager

Apps that are new in your device before will need permission for the first-time usage, the app must have permission before you can use the Camera, Microphone, or Location.

1. Launch the Settings application to get started then tap ⊙ Privacy and select Permission manager.
2. Select a category then tap a program to select the permission you want to be notified about.

Samsung Privacy

If you are having a technical problem on your Phone, you can send diagnostic details about your phone to Samsung.

1. Open the Settings app as the starting point then tap 🔘 Privacy.
2. Choose an option to customize under Samsung:
- Samsung Privacy: View the privacy info of Samsung.
- Customization Service: Samsung can be allowed to produced customized content and suggestions.
- Send diagnostic data: You can send info to be diagnosed about your phone to Samsung if technical issues are occurring on your device.

Date and time

To set the time manually or automatically, follow the easy steps below.

- Go to the Settings app and click the 🔘 General management icon to get started> then select Date and time. The options below are:

- Automatic date and time: On normal operation circumstances of your device, date and time updates are received from your wireless network. You will see the following options are available if automatic date and time is disabled:
  - Select time zone: Pick a new time zone from the list of time zones.
  - Set date: Enter the current date.
  - Set time: Enter the current time of the day.
- Use 24-hour format: Choose the format of displaying time.

Reset

All settings on your Samsung A15 Smartphone can be reset.

Reset all settings

To reset all settings to the device's factory default, do the following:

NOTE: Your personal will not be harmed.

1. From the Starting point (Settings), click 🎛 General management, tap Reset and then tap Reset all settings.

2. Select Reset settings

3. Follow the instruction showing on the screen.

Reset network settings

Network settings can also be reset to it default

1. Launch the Start page (Settings) and select ⚙ General management and tap Reset then select Reset network settings.

2. Select Reset network settings, and confirm.

Reset accessibility settings

To reset accessibility settings, you must have it in mind that all your downloaded application and personal data are not affected.

1. Launch the Settings application to begin then select the ⚙ General management option and tap "Reset" then click on "Reset accessibility settings".

2. Touch "Reset accessibility setting" and confirm.

Auto restart at set times

Your Samsung A15 device can be set to restart at a particular time

NOTE: If your device restarts unsaved data cannot be recovered

1. Launch the Settings app to start this process and tap the ☰ General management menu the tap "Reset" and lastly "Auto restart at set times".
2. To turn on the Auto restart, touch ⬤ then set the options below:

- Days: Set the particular day of the week you want your device to restart.
- Time: Set the particular time of the day you want your device to reset.

Factory Data Reset

Performing a factory data reset on your device will erase all its data including, music, videos, pictures, Google account and other settings. Only files stored on an external SD card will not be deleted.

Before resetting your phone:

1. Verify that all the data you want to retain has been moved your external storage area.
2. Login to your Google Account and confirm your user name and password.

To reset your phone:

1. Go to the Settings page to start the process and tap ⬚ General management > Reset > Factory data reset.
2. Click Reset and follow the on the screen prompt to perform the reset.
3. If the phone restarts, follow the on-screen instruction to set up your phone.

Google Device Protection

This feature will be activated when you login to your Google account and set up a lock screen. This feature protects your gadget form non-permitted factory data rest by requesting your Google account info to confirm your identity.

Enable Google Device Protection

To enable "Google Device Protection" you must login to a Google account and set a lock screen.

Disable Google Device Protection

Remove all Google accounts that are signed in on your device to deactivate the Google Device Protection features.

To remove Google accounts:

1. Launch the Setting apps to get started and select the 🔄 Accounts and backup option> then tap Manage accounts > [Google Account].
2. Select Remove account.

To remove a secure Lock screen:

1. Launch the Setting app to get started and select 🔒 Lock screen > then tap Screen lock type.
2. Select None or Swipe.

www.ingramcontent.com/pod-product-compliance
Lightning Source LLC
Chambersburg PA
CBHW070241230526
45470CB00002B/469